THE
SIMPLE
SHIFT

THE
SIMPLE
SHIFT

HOW USEFUL THINKING CHANGES THE WAY YOU SEE EVERYTHING

CHRIS HELDER

WILEY

First published in 2020 by John Wiley & Sons Australia, Ltd
42 McDougall St, Milton Qld 4064

Office also in Melbourne

Typeset in Sabon LT Std 11/15 pt

© John Wiley & Sons Australia, Ltd 2020

The moral rights of the author have been asserted

ISBN: 978-0-730-38166-2

A catalogue record for this book is available from the National Library of Australia

Cover design by Wiley

Cover image © beakraus / Getty Images

Printed in Singapore by Markono Print Media Pte Ltd

10 9 8 7 6 5 4 3 2 1

Disclaimer

The material in this publication is of the nature of general comment only, and does not represent professional advice. It is not intended to provide specific guidance for particular circumstances and it should not be relied on as the basis for any decision to take action or not take action on any matter which it covers. Readers should obtain professional advice where appropriate, before making any such decision. To the maximum extent permitted by law, the author and publisher disclaim all responsibility and liability to any person, arising directly or indirectly from any person taking or not taking action based on the information in this publication.

The best way to read this book

Much like *Useful Belief*, the best way to read this book is from start to finish, ideally in one sitting. It might only take you a plane flight.

The whole book is a journey and each section runs seamlessly into the next.

However, you will find a contents list on the next page if you find yourself searching again for a particular part.

Contents

About Chris Helder

Chris Helder is a world-class keynote speaker and master storyteller. His presentations have radically changed how thousands of people worldwide communicate and deal with adversity.

Chris has presented over 2500 times around the world during his 18 year speaking career.

He is the author of three best-selling books:

» *Useful Belief*—one of the highest selling Australian business books of all time
» *The Ultimate Book of Influence*—which has been published in five languages
» *Cut The Noise*—which is about achieving better results in a world of distraction

Introduction

Life can be overwhelming.

I was in my hotel room just before Christmas and one of the morning shows was playing on the television. Of course they are always chasing the next sensational headline, and their guest that day was the latest in a seemingly never-ending roll call of health and fitness gurus, every one looking to make more noise than the last. Tuning in, I heard him say, 'We are actually not advocating stretching anymore …'

What? Really? I do stretches every day. That's it, I'm out!

Every day it's something different. A new idea that utterly contradicts what was being advocated just a couple of weeks ago!

I mean, seriously. It's impossible to keep up. I remember when I was supposed to 'carb load' to boost my energy levels for the day. Not anymore! Now we're told carbohydrates are evil. Then the trend was towards eating only meat. Eat like the caveman, they said. Yeah, that sounds like a good idea, let's emulate the caveman. Because if he was lucky he might have lived to be all of 32 years old. Then it was fruit. Eat only fruit. All day. Then we got right down to it and just drank the juice. Everyone in Australia bought a juicer. The problem was, the fruit was full of sugar, and everyone knows sugar is bad for you!

Think about how breakfast has changed. I was always taught that eating a good, hearty breakfast set you up for the day. Not anymore! Now there are some who will advise you to stop eating at 6 pm and fast until noon the next day, or to eat five days a week and fast for the other two. I don't know, now they have me on ketones and putting butter in my coffee!

The world is full of noise, yet no matter how much it annoys us, we are addicted to it. Every day brings a complete overload of information that's impossible to keep up with. We all experience it, respond to it, even relish it. Sometimes I can't believe the things I click on. In a corner of my mind I think and worry about the profile 'they' are building up of me, as I skip from a provocative *Daily Mail* headline to a famous sports personality's drug addiction to the latest celebrity wardrobe malfunction.

One challenge is constant comparison. The relentless messaging that we need to be somehow better, fitter, stronger, smarter, more attractive. At every turn the media are telling us we're not good enough. Of course, this is on top of the fact that we are all to some degree addicted to the dopamine hit we experience when we receive any affirmation, such as through our likes on social media. We are addicted to feedback and the approval of others. This is well documented and is not going to change anytime soon.

We are told we live in the greatest time in human history. Is that true? Well, it's complicated.

So maybe we need to simplify it.

There are certainly strong arguments to be made that it is the most complicated time in human history. While most of us are pretty safe from contracting the plague or being cut down by raiders from a neighbouring village, we nonetheless suffer the highest levels of depression, anxiety and general unhappiness in recorded history.

Despite the thousands of books teaching us how to be mentally and physically healthy, mainly through doing the things we have always done—eat food, have babies, raise children, exercise and pursue healthy activities, and communicate with other human beings—it turns out we are less healthy and, what's more, clearly less happy than ever. With so many more choices, life has become much more complicated.

The purpose of this book is to cut through that complexity, all that noise, and to introduce you to a simple, practical philosophy that encourages you to live your life with a greater focus on what is useful. We'll explore useful things for you to believe to increase the possibilities of joy in your life. This is an idea that creates its own momentum. It will guide you towards identifying what is useful in your life and what is simply noise. It will help you figure out what you need to do and what you need to delegate or avoid. It will help you identify what matters and what doesn't.

It will help guide some readers through significant adversity in their lives, while helping others create a strategy for infusing that mundane Monday meeting with greater energy. For many, it will be the call to action they have been looking for to create massive change in their lives.

This is my manifesto. My philosophy for navigating the craziness and the wonder of the modern world. It's a simple, powerful idea that opens up limitless possibility for all of us.

Evolving useful belief

I wrote my first book, *Useful Belief*, as a fable. The narrator travels from Melbourne to a conference in Barcelona and meets three people along the way. One is a woman from his past; another is a young businessman who challenges his understanding of how the younger generation differ from previous ones; and the last is a middle-aged speaker who kicks off the Barcelona conference, sharing her own story with a rapt audience. These three encounters change his perspective on life in a profound way.

Useful Belief, like the book you're holding now, is a quick and easy read that conveys a simple idea, but this single simple idea has the power to trigger a shift that changes how you see *everything*. That book has become one of the biggest selling business books in Australia.

Why write another book about 'useful belief'? Easy. The simple idea has evolved. Since that book's publication I have had the chance to share the idea on stage with thousands of people, and their feedback has been amazing. I have given a TEDx talk on the subject. People have sent me photos of them reading the book in extraordinary places all over the world, such as in front of the Eiffel Tower, floating down the Red Sea and on a warship in the middle of the ocean.

I love what I do. This inspirational idea has allowed me to present to such a variety of industries and organisations that it sometimes leaves me shaking my head in wonder. I have been the keynote speaker at conferences featuring financial service providers, planners, brokers, lawyers, doctors, people involved in the pharmaceutical, skin care and hair care industries, real estate, sales of all kinds, customer service and the military. The journey has been humbling and wonderful. I don't think I fully recognised when I wrote the book that the idea applied equally to *everyone*. Every industry. Every business. Every person.

I am often described as a motivational speaker, but I really don't like the title. I think it labels me in a way that somehow suggests I'm not a regular person, when the fact is I'm dealing with a lot of the same stuff as everyone else. We are all riding this thing called life. We all have to deal with obligations and commitments around financial, business, relationship, parenting, family, friends, health and countless other concerns.

Over the past 18 years I have presented to well over 2500 audiences. I have seen how many people expend endless energy worrying about or trying to change things they have absolutely no control over.

This book is about making a simple shift in your thinking. A simple shift that will help you focus on what is truly useful in order to make the most of your life. You will learn how useful thinking outperforms positive thinking. Positive thinking is based on emotions, which go up and down. Useful thinking is practical, pragmatic and focused, and it delivers results. If you have challenges right now, deciding to 'be positive' won't fix them. Useful thinking and strategy will.

This book will show you how to frame your challenges so you can better meet and overcome them. It will help you formulate an action plan based on where you need to be. Above all, it will teach you how a simple shift will change how you see everything.

Transformation doesn't usually work

I have always been frustrated by speakers, books and programs that promise to 'transform' you. 'Come to our weekend seminar and you will leave a new person!' My experience is that these programs don't create lasting change in most people. It is like deciding to transform your body when you are unfit by going to the gym four days in a row and running 20 miles a day and lifting full weights. You won't be transformed; you will be broken. More than that, I actually don't think most people need to be completely transformed. Rather, they need to make a simple shift in the way they perceive the world. Useful belief and useful thinking are all about simple shifts that open the possibilities in your life.

'Focus on your goal *with every cell in your body*,' they insist fervently, or 'Focus on your goal with every part of your DNA!' How do you do that? What does it even mean? These motivational clichés are actually damaging because they set people up to fail, so they end up feeling worse about themselves than when they started. Useful belief and useful thinking involve simple shifts, and once on your new trajectory you will find your life has changed.

Positive thinking doesn't really work

Motivational speakers typically urge us to be positive. Our parents and teachers told us the same thing. I was at a Christmas party once and this guy walked up (I think he'd had a couple of drinks), looked at me and said, 'I hear you're a motivational speaker. Why don't you say something right now to motivate me.'

'It doesn't work like that,' I said.

'So what *do* you do?' he demanded. 'Do you stand in front of people and just tell them in your American accent to *be positive*? Is that what you say?'

I knew he was poking the bear. I understood that. And at the same time he did have a point. And it was probably pretty much the same thing you're asking right now. Is there something new out there, something different from all that positive thinking stuff?

Well, here we go. Idea number one. Positive thinking doesn't really work.

But Chris, positive thinking is a staple of modern motivation theory.

Well no. The fact is, studies show it doesn't work. Not really. For example, if you've been in a rut for the past six days, six weeks or six months, positive thinking won't get you out of it. If you are anticipating being in a rut for the next six days, six weeks or six months, positive thinking won't help you move forward.

Imagine if you are in a bad mood at work and someone walks up to you and says, 'Hey, come on! Pull yourself out of it. Be positive!' How would you like to respond?

Boom.

That's just not going to work. It's not going to produce a positive outcome. In the same way, you may lie in bed in the morning and tell yourself, *Come on, I can do this. Today will be a good day if I just try to keep positive*... Again, the studies show that by 10 o'clock, when something bad happens, you're no longer able to sustain that level of positive thinking, and you end up feeling worse about yourself than when you started. *I can't even do positive well.*

So, 'No, I don't teach positive thinking,' I told my interrogator at the Christmas party. 'I teach useful thinking. Because if you're in a rut, positive won't get you out of it. Useful will.'

If, for whatever reason, you feel like you are at ground zero in your life, the question you need to ask is, what is the most useful thing you can do to get from zero to two? Then what is the most useful action for you to take to get from two to five? What about getting from five to eight?

To progress, you need to think about what is the most useful thing for you to believe about your reality? This thinking leads you to discover what is really important and to get results. Let's take a look at a couple of real-life examples.

This is the greatest time to be ... anything

Since the dawn of time, the older generation has loved to take shots at the younger. It's nothing new — it's always been like that. For those readers with a few grey hairs, how often have you heard these complaints: 'I can't believe these kids today. Constantly staring at their iPhones and computer games. When I was young, we had a real childhood. We were active, outside kids. We took off on our bikes, or with a bat and ball, and we ran around till Mum called us in for dinner. We lived outside.'

Have you ever been a part of this conversation? Every now and then people ask me about what I think about 'kids today'. Well, I have three teenage boys so I guess I'm qualified to offer an answer ...

Hmm ... let me see. Let's try this. I think this is the greatest time in the history of the world to be a kid. I think it is the most fantastic time in history to be a dad, a parent. What do you think? Do you think that's true?

I have no idea if it's true or not. Really, how could we possibly know? So, maybe it's true. But is it useful? *Definitely!*

'Truth' can sometimes be overrated. I mean, it really comes down to your perception. If you choose to believe that something is true, you can find plenty of evidence to support it. As a child you were taught all sorts of things were true. As you got older and looked back at those things with the benefit of an adult brain, you discovered that not only were many of them not true, but some were quite ridiculous.

So I don't know if it's necessarily true that this is the most fantastic time to be alive, but I know it's useful to think so. Because when I believe it is the best time in the history of the world to be a dad, the most amazing thing happens: *I'm a better dad.* I'm actually dialled into what is happening this year, not focused on that Def Leppard concert I went to in 1989. I'm right here, right now.

The same holds true of my view of the world today. Is it the best time ever to be alive? Is that true? The media certainly suggests it's not. But here's the thing: if you believe it is, an amazing thing happens. You walk outside and what

This is the greatest time to be ... anything

do you see? You see a tree, a flower, a puppy, a baby! You find beautiful things everywhere.

But how does this work? Let's stop for a second and look at the simple science behind useful belief. The most important part of your brain when it comes to your personal success in life is called the reticular activating system.

What's that? The reticular activating system is your brain's filter. It filters the millions of pieces of information available to you every day and decides what you actually get to see and experience. We can come up with an easier way to see what it does. Some call it the 'Red Toyota Theory'. Just for the record, last year in Australia I presented at conferences for Mercedes, Honda and Holden, so I diplomatically changed the name. They did not want to hear about Toyotas!

Here's how it works. If I asked you how many red Toyotas you saw the last time you took a drive, you'd probably reply that as far as you can recall you didn't see any. That's at least partly because you weren't looking for red Toyotas. If you've just made the decision to buy a red Toyota, however, then the next time you're out on the road you'll be spotting red Toyotas everywhere you look.

Because now you're dialled in to red Toyotas. That's your reticular activating system at work.

So how does this relate to our view of the world? Let's get back to our useful belief that this is the best time in the history of the world to be alive. If you believe this you'll find beautiful things everywhere. If you believe it is the best time ever to be a parent, you will be more present, in the here and now, and be a better parent, excited about the events and happenings in your child's world.

This is the greatest time to be ... anything

Times are tough, if you let them be

Not everyone believes these are the best of times, though. I get that. Some people would rather dwell on the tough realities, and these are definitely, unprecedentedly tough times.

If you want to subscribe to this perspective, I want to support you as well. Some people love to be unhappy and want to stay that way. If this is you, I do have some good news for you. You will have a lot of friends. You will probably enjoy minimal personal success, but on the plus side you will have lots of people at the office with whom to discuss the seriousness of these tough times. You will find plenty of support in those coffee machine conversations, because misery does love company. When you are convinced these are tough times, your reticular activating system will find terrible things everywhere.

Here are some recommendations on how you can help support your world view on tough times. First, dial in to a lot of news programs. In fact, take in as much media in general as possible. Watch all those tabloid journalism shows that come on after the news. This will help cement your view of humanity. Also watch as much reality television as you can. Make sure you go online to read all the articles about the reality TV personalities to help you form your own view on what healthy relationships look like. Oh, and try to get all your financial advice from the same newspaper that carries the betting odds for the footy.

Following this regime will increase your general paranoia about the society we live in and will help you form irrational viewpoints on everything from immigration to why your household appliances are actually slowly killing you!

Times are tough, if you let them be

Life begins at 70

A couple of years ago I had the chance to present at a conference in Las Vegas. The conference was put on for 20 of the top real estate agents in the United States, 10 men and 10 women. I was going to be presenting to this room of uber-successful people on the subject of (you guessed it) useful belief. Let me tell you there were a few egos in that room!

When I first walked into the room an older gentleman spotted me and called out, 'Chris Helder is here! Life begins at 70!'

A little disconcerted, I smiled at him and he motioned me to the door leading out into the hallway.

'Chris, let me introduce myself. I heard you talk at a conference where you said that life begins at 70 years old. That's what you said, Chris Helder. Now, I'm 74 years old and I want you to guess how old I was when I started my real estate business. Go on, have a guess.'

'Well...I'll take a guess that you were maybe 40 years old.'

'I was not,' he shot back happily. 'I was in fact 70 years old. That's right, 70. I'd had no previous experience of real estate, and now, just four years later, I have 110 people working under me. I'm sitting in a room with 19 of the top realtors in the US and I want you to know something, Chris Helder. You *need* to know this. I sell Florida!'

I love it. He took the whole damned state.

Life begins at 70 is a useful belief if you are 70. Life begins at 40 is a useful belief if you are 40, but not if you are 70. Life begins at 22 is a useful belief if you are 22, when you'll say, 'Of course it does ... look at me!'

I hear people say all the time, 'I look old. I feel old. I am old.' But you know what? This is the best time ever to be you. Now, I don't mean to be the bearer of bad news, but the survival rate on this planet is exactly zero per cent. None of us is getting out of here alive! I don't mean this in a negative way, but it's a useful thought. Given that you're going to be nothing more than a paragraph on ancestory.com in 100 years' time, you may as well make the most of the time you have. This is the best time in the history of the world to live. Is it true? I don't know, but it's useful.

And I want to say this: you look good today. You do. I could actually prove it to you. I could take a photograph of you right now, and I could show you *that* photo in 10 years' time, and you'd look at it and say, 'Awww, I looked good. Look how young I am there.' So given that you're going to feel that way 10 years from now anyway, you may as well go with that as a useful belief now. You look good today!

This is the best time ever to be alive, to be a parent, to be in your business, your industry. There are opportunities everywhere. Life begins at (insert your current age) and you look good today. With these useful beliefs on board, your brain is going to start opening to the possibilities of your life.

How to come up with useful beliefs

How do you identify your own most useful beliefs? This is where the process of useful thinking comes in. I want to dig in and challenge you on the life you have created for yourself. Some readers may wake up and feel great about almost every aspect of their lives. That's fantastic! Most likely, though, many more will find themselves facing multiple frustrations. They feel overwhelmed and trapped by circumstances they are unable to change. That's okay. We're going to talk about that.

Which brings me to another frustration: the speakers (or books or inspirational quotes) that urge people to ignore the realities they face and chase unrealistic dreams. These speakers tell inspiring stories of travelling the globe in search of adventure and enlightenment, and they encourage their audience to chase their dreams as they have. 'Dream great dreams and you can achieve great things—just as I have!' is their message. 'You can take the next three months and go find yourself,' they say.

In the meantime, many in the audience are thinking, 'Easy for him to say. He doesn't have my obligations. I wish I had the freedom to just drop everything to go find myself. But I have a job, three kids, a mortgage and car payments to keep up. I'd love to do something like that, but I just can't.' Whether the constraints are financial, family or fear, most people have obligations they can't simply set aside to go chase exciting experiences.

The best speakers and authors in this space will share their amazing journey then spend time drawing out takeaways in the form of practical, realistic advice to help people in their everyday lives. Sometimes life is challenging. Sometimes bad things happen. What's important is how you frame your reality and the bad things that happen.

I'm sure from time to time we all imagine living some perfect life that is completely unattainable. It's fun to dream. I want to focus on equipping you with the power to deal with every level of adversity you might face.

Useful thinking has two applications. First I'm going to share with you a method for making decisions in your life by using useful thinking. It might actually be the way we should make all the big decisions in our lives. It's pretty amazing how much clarity it can bring. I hope you like it. Afterwards I will introduce some examples of how useful thinking allows you to come up with the useful beliefs to deal with your reality, the good stuff and the bad. Bad things happen to good people. Useful thinking will give you a way to navigate through the challenges you will inevitably face.

Of course, traditionally people have made decisions based on a combination of emotion, logic and input from other people. While the useful thinking method doesn't remove those influences from the process, it does focus on the story you are going to tell *after* you make the decision. It's about determining which story actually sits better with you.

Since human beings first rose up and walked on two feet they have had decisions to make. Do I go left? Do I go right? Should I fight or run? Useful thinking will guide you towards a useful belief. Let's explore what this means.

How to come up with useful beliefs

Here is a three-part process for making any decision by analysing the story we tell or, more specifically, the useful belief we have no matter what decision we make. Here we go:

1. Consider your situation

It is important to discover some clarity about how you feel about the things that are happening in your life. For example, I was working through a scenario with a CEO friend of mine who had been offered a role that would see him in Sydney four days a week. The money was better and the opportunities were huge. These factors were compelling, but it was also worth considering that he lives in Melbourne and has three teenage children. So the change would have a huge impact on his family.

2. Think usefully

Here's where you identify all your relevant useful beliefs and determine which one will sit best with the current reality. This is the decision-making process of useful thinking. The useful beliefs that came up in conversation with my CEO friend included:

> This is a once-in-a-lifetime opportunity. I am making the right decision. Everyone will have to sacrifice a bit, but that will be okay. It will build resilience in the kids, and that will keep our relationships fresh. There will be more money to do more things, so we can have more quality time when we are together.

Or...

> The timing isn't right. There will be other opportunities. Right now, family is my priority. I won't get these years back. This is the best time ever to be a dad and I'm not going to miss out on it.

The CEO could make either decision now. There is no right answer. The reality is that both options are perfectly valid. Most of the toughest questions in our lives have multiple legitimate answers. This is where useful thinking comes into play. This is not about thinking how you 'feel' about each scenario. Rather, and this is most important, it is

How to come up with useful beliefs

about finding the useful belief that sits best with you. What is the useful belief that you will live with? What story are you going to tell? What belief is strongest? The decision becomes clear when you focus on the useful belief you have identified instead of the emotion of that decision.

3. Decide on a useful belief

Useful thinking is the process of working through the possible useful beliefs to determine the best solution based on your current reality. This is much stronger than going back and forth with an emotional decision. Should I? Shouldn't I? Once you have determined the useful belief that sits best with you, then you can make your decision with confidence.

Then be okay with the decision. Think about the difference. When you face a situation that can throw up multiple correct decisions, the best way to achieve clarity is to go to the story you feel best about. What is the useful belief that sits best with you? There you have your answer.

We all have our own reality

Many readers will not be happy with the current state of their life. I get that. So please don't imagine this is a philosophy that is all rainbows, unicorns and butterflies. I'm not saying you don't face challenges. We all do. For every single person reading this book, reality can be demanding, even harsh.

Of course, you could change that reality right now. You could finish reading this book and start spending a lot of time on vanlife.com.au. You could pack up and go buy a camper van. You could drive that van up to the Top End and settle in to a life on the beach. You could do it, grow your hair back out and smoke the good stuff in the back of the van. You could get out there and create an entirely new reality!

For some of you that might sound tempting. Some may have already taken out their life savings to go buy the van. Many people dream wildly about the changes they think they would like to make in their life. Those dreams might involve changing their job or career, starting a new business, leaving their current relationship, selling the house, simplifying their life, making a sea change, a tree change or maybe just a me change. Here's the thing though: if you're going to change it, you'll need a useful belief about it.

What are your useful beliefs about your reality?

There are actually two things that will block your personal and professional growth this year.

The first is focusing on or complaining about things you can't control. You know this. Focusing on things that are beyond your power to influence is like banging your head against the wall. I live in Melbourne. What a waste of energy it would be for me to complain about the weather. 'I can't believe this rain. I can't believe that we get all four seasons during the first quarter of the footy. I can't believe that in summer it's 45 degrees one day then 16 the next!'

That simply would not be useful. I live in this city and I'm not moving right now. There is a reality concerning the weather that I could change: I could move to somewhere with a different climate. If I'm not going to move, though,

I may as well have a useful belief about the thing I can't control. So, I love Melbourne weather. I love the variety, the surprises. I love all the seasons! You get the idea.

The second thing that will stop you growing this year is actually even more important to dial in to. That is focusing on, complaining about, carrying on about things you *will* not change. You can usually change your reality. But if you're not going to change it, then you may as well have a useful belief about that.

How often do you go to meetings that are a complete waste of time? We all have to do it. We are required to attend and can't get out of it. It's so easy in these situations to turn to a colleague and say, 'I can't believe we have to go to this meeting. It's going to be a total waste of time.'

So what behaviour do most people fall into? They show up at the meeting, plunk themselves down and cross their arms resentfully. Then they send their brain (the reticular activating system) on a fact-finding mission in search of proof that the meeting is really a waste of time.

If you have to go to the meeting, and you can't get out of it, do some useful thinking to come up with a useful belief.

We all have our own reality

Be open. Who knows, you may actually learn something that sparks a useful idea. Yes, the meeting may end up being a waste of time for you, but since you are going anyway, you may as well approach it with a useful belief.

We all have our own reality. For many married women every day starts with waking up and finding the same person lying next to them. Day in and day out, that same person is taking up space on the other side of the bed. Some days they may think to themselves, 'I'm going to look over there in a minute and it's not going to be him today. Today it's going to be Bradley Cooper. Counting down, 3 … 2 … 1 … Nope. It's still him.'

We all have a reality. If you can't change it or won't change it, you may as well come up with a useful belief about it.

My reality

I have a reality as a professional speaker. Travel is a big part of that reality. Last year I gave 159 presentations, flew on 156 airplanes and stayed in hotels an even 110 nights. I did all of that in 12 months. That's a lot of travel.

When I share those statistics with audiences they are amazed. People will approach me afterwards and offer comments wrapped in sympathy and concern: 'Wow, Chris, you must hate all that travel. I know I would. All those hotels. Being alone all the time.' People love to say such things to me about my reality.

I *could* change it, too. Simple. I could just do Melbourne gigs. That would solve it. No more travel.

Except for a couple of problems: It would affect my income and it would affect my lifestyle. Most of all, though, I don't want to. I love what I do! I love public speaking. So you know what? I'm not going to change it. And if I'm not going to change it, I may as well have a useful belief about it. What's my useful belief about travel?

I love airplanes! I love them! I love airports and airport lounges. I love relaxing in the Qantas lounge or the Virgin lounge, enjoying the free food they offer, and I *really* love the ham they serve in both those lounges. Actually, I have a little conspiracy theory I'd like to share with you right now. I believe Qantas and Virgin *share* their ham. I believe we have a shared ham situation going on at airports around Australia. But I love it!

And I love hotels and hotel sheets. I am alone a lot of the time. Walking the streets of Sydney … alone. Walking along Main Beach on the Gold Coast … alone. Walking around the Alamo in San Antonio, Texas … alone, alone. And do you know what I love? Aloneness. I love being alone.

By the way, if you are out there and feeling lonely. Don't dial in to lonely. There's no power in that. Dial in to *aloneness*. There is power in aloneness. This is the best time in the history of the world to be alone. Imagine being alone in the year 1722, freezing in some thatched-roof shack in the north of England at three o'clock in the morning, knitting by candlelight. It surely would have been a miserable time to be alone. Now there are a million things to do at three o'clock in the morning! This is the best time ever to power up with some aloneness.

Focus on what you can control

In every audience I speak to there will likely be someone who is not open to receiving my message, for whatever reason. People show up at conferences and events with a lot going on in both their personal and professional lives. Someone may be weighed down by huge work pressure and feelings of complete overwhelm. Someone else may arrive having just had an argument with their spouse and may be too distracted to participate. Another may arrive burdened with a strong prejudice based on past experiences. They may be thinking, 'I am *not* going to listen to this guy. I have had too many bad experiences with short American men. I'm not going down that path again, Chris Helder. Been there, done that!'

I am well aware that it is totally possible there are people in the audience who are not in a good place for being open and receptive to new ideas. The reality is that there is nothing I can do to *control* that for them. And I'm also totally okay with that. As we've established, I am not going to spend time focused on things I can't control. So that's really on them. Instead, I'm going to focus on the one thing I can control, which is my output. That's it. It's the one thing we can all control every day. Our output. How we show up.

I promise you one thing. It doesn't matter how many people are in the audience, I'll show up with a useful belief and give you everything I've got.

The heart doesn't judge

Useful belief can take many forms depending on what is actually driving the thinking behind it. For example, success is a very subjective idea. You can create a belief system that is about personal success and at the same time be a really good person. You can create beliefs about helping others and achieve great results doing that. By the same token, you can create a belief system that is successful but also somewhat damaging: it may achieve results, but it may be driven by selfish behaviour and narcissism.

You can create some powerful, ego-driven useful beliefs. It might mean faking it until you make it—that can be a useful belief. Or it might involve a little bit of irrational confidence—certainly that has been a successful strategy for some. Sometimes people are trying to prove themselves to be better than everyone else, which can be a huge driving factor for success. The need to win, defeat others and prove to yourself that you are the best has been a significant driver in many of the greatest success stories of our society.

In addition, some people can drive successful useful beliefs from a place of anger. How often have you heard about the person from the wrong side of the tracks who was determined to use their childhood pain to fuel the fire. A relentless passion to succeed driven by anger has been a catalyst for many of our culture's most successful people.

Ego and anger. They can be useful to create outcomes.

That said, how do you get the most out of the useful beliefs in your life? What kind of belief delivers the most powerful holistic results? The answer is obvious and simple. Useful belief works best when it is driven from the heart, not the ego. It is most powerful when it is driven from authenticity, not anger.

Let me pull an example from my own speaking career. Being a speaker is a very vulnerable occupation. Early in my career there were definitely audiences that I was fearful of when preparing to step onstage. You get a feel for a room when you walk in. Sometimes the conferences were boring and the audiences resentful. When the organisation had an obviously toxic culture, the audience might look extremely unhappy. It could be pretty scary.

The useful belief I would choose would be a survival technique. I would pump up my ego and tell myself how they were lucky to have me speak today. I would draw on an irrational confidence to tell myself I was the smartest person in the room. Also, I would feel my anger kick in. *I'll show them*, I would think. *Look out ... here I come!*

Ego and anger. And they did help me. They were useful.

My approach is very different now, though. Today I'll think about how I'm feeling and what's going on for me. I may be feeling vulnerable because of the boring conference or the organisation's evidently toxic culture. That's okay. I'll summon a useful belief from the heart. It may sound something like this: *I'm feeling nervous and vulnerable, but that's okay. I have no doubt there are others in this room who are also feeling vulnerable today. I can help them. I'm going to go onstage and deliver my best presentation. I can't control the reaction, but I'm going to give them everything I've got.*

My presentation comes out better when driven from the heart. No chip on my shoulder, I'm driving from a place of love. I'm driving from the heart.

How do I know if I'm driving from the heart? Simple. The heart doesn't judge. You know you are driving from a place of ego or anger if you are judging others. You know you are driving from the heart if you are accepting others.

Drive your business from the heart.

Energy is a decision

While we're talking about driving from the heart, let's talk about energy. One of the things I am most recognised for as a professional speaker is my energy level. Energy is a very big part of my business plan. In fact, this can be a big point of difference between you and your competitors. At conferences I often hear of the team's efforts to identify their unique selling proposition. They get out the flipcharts and the markers and try desperately to identify the main differences between them and the competition. I recommend starting with this: *Out-energise the competition.* Energy is a decision.

This useful belief has become a catchphrase at my presentations. Energy is a decision, a choice. You can draw on as much energy as you want. Most people don't subscribe to this view. Most people are tired, even exhausted. If you doubt this, just walk up and ask them, and they will tell you how tired they are. You probably already had this conversation today.

'How are you today?'

'Yeah, pretty good. I'm just tired, man, just a little tired.'

'Why are you tired?'

'I don't know. I got 10 hours' sleep last night. I've just been so busy.'

Young people are no different. Rubbing their eyes they respond, 'Oh, I don't know. I'm 25 and I've got the rest of my life ahead of me, but I'm exhausted.'

Energy is a choice. You can have as much as you want. *I am an energetic person.* That's your line, by the way.

But here's the thing I am most proud of: in 2500 presentations I have *never* shown up without an abundance of energy. Energy is a decision. I don't care if there are 12 people or 5000 people in the audience. Those people are giving me the gift of their time, so it is my job to show up with an abundance of energy. Energy is a choice and you can show up with as much as you want.

People ask me, 'Chris, how do I find that level of energy?'

The answer is very simple. Get connected to your life. When you are connected to your life, you will find stacks of energy. When you are disconnected from your life, you are constantly tired.

That, of course, begs the next question. How do you get connected to your life?

Once again the answer is simple. Make sure you have a useful belief about the things you can't or won't change. Or change them!

You have your reality. We all have our reality. For me, it's the best time in the history of the world to get stuck in traffic. There are podcasts to listen to that allow you to learn and grow while you drive. You used to get stuck in traffic with nothing but a few crappy radio stations to listen to. This is the best time in the history of the world to have a three-hour layover in Dallas. There are endless shopping, restaurant and people-watching opportunities. Imagine layovers 40 years ago. There would have been nowhere but a seedy airport bar to pass the time in.

Recently a friend of mine in Sydney told me she was having lunch with her two best friends when I popped into her head.

'I did? Why?' I asked.

'Well,' she said. 'Something happened at the restaurant that would normally have made me quite angry. I usually would have got fired up and made a big deal of it.'

'What happened?' I asked, intrigued.

'When they brought out my food and set it down, I noticed a long, black hair on the plate. Normally I would have made a scene, but then suddenly I heard your voice.'

'Go on.'

'I just heard you say, "I love hair in my food!" And you know what, I had a bit of a giggle to myself and just removed the hair. Because it really wasn't a big deal.'

She thought it useful not to make a scene and upset the lunch. Probably not what I had in mind, but interesting though. If we start thinking about all the things we get so upset about, is any of it actually worth it? Is it worth expending all that energy on things that don't really matter. Energy is a choice, and where you direct your energy is also a choice. Think about the useful things you could direct your energy towards, then the things that are really not important that you sink huge amounts of energy into.

You control the amount of energy you have and how you distribute and utilise that energy. All of this hinges on useful belief. Remember, you are an energetic person. You are completely in control of your own energy and how you utilise it.

Life is full of challenges

I had just finished presenting at a conference in Adelaide when a woman approached me and shared with me how she had suffered anxiety and depression her whole life. She was 28 years old. Her family had always urged her to be happier and more positive, but mostly she didn't *feel* happy. She didn't *feel* positive. When she attended one of my presentations and heard me say, 'Positive thinking doesn't work', she said she felt as though the weight of the world had been lifted off her shoulders. She no longer had to 'be positive'.

Three months later she called me and told me that an amazing thing had happened. She wanted to give me an update on how her life had changed since she had embraced the idea of useful belief. She told me she woke up every day now and asked herself one question: 'What are the most useful things for me to do today to get through the day?'

The result? First, she told me, she had never got more done. She had never been more productive in her entire life. That was pretty cool. The second thing she hadn't expected, though. She found she was now happier than she had ever been before.

Happiness isn't actually something to try to achieve. Rather, it is the result of living a full life, a useful life, and of being *connected* to your life.

Here's another example. I once received an email from a man who had suffered an accident a year before that left him with burns covering a third of his body. He told me how he had spent the past year grieving over his injuries. Who could blame him? But the photo that accompanied that email showed him, just out of surgery, holding a copy of a book he had been given—*Useful Belief*. He was done grieving now, he said. The grieving process was normal and had even been useful, but he knew there was nothing he could do to change what had happened—that is, to change his reality. Now it was time to move on and to work on a useful belief for the rest of his life.

We all have bad things happen to us in our lives. For some, like my email friend, these can be devastating. His life will never be the same, but that doesn't mean it can't be amazing.

Many people get sick. Yet, given the amazing advances in medicine and technology, for most of us it is surely the best time in history to be sick, since in any earlier age many of the medical conditions that are relatively easy to treat today would often have proved fatal. Today we have much greater knowledge and resources for treating disease than at any time in history. That is a useful belief.

Really bad things still happen to really good people, but useful belief will help you deal with those bad things.

People often ask me how I came up with the useful belief idea. It should come as no surprise to hear that it happened during an international flight. I was on my way from San Francisco to Sydney, and for once the trip wasn't work related. I was coming back from my father's funeral.

I was feeling incredibly anxious on that journey, because while I was still dealing with my grief, I also knew I had to deliver 18 presentations around Australia over the following four weeks. I can tell you that, for sure, I didn't want to do that. I didn't feel motivated, and I certainly didn't feel like motivating anyone else. I felt angry and very, very sad.

I am a habitual journal writer and I was writing in my journal about my feelings around getting through the next four weeks. My pen flew across each page as I gave vent to the pain I felt inside. My writing was so angry that I was filling most pages with just a couple of sentences. On one I scrawled from one side of the page to the other in huge letters, '*I need a new belief!!! This is not useful!!!*'

I looked down at what I had written and those two words leapt off the page. And suddenly I felt I had stumbled on a truly valuable idea. When I got to Sydney I googled them and discovered that no one else appeared to have made the association before me, I began to warm to the idea even more!

What happened next was amazing. I came up with a useful belief to get me through the next four stressful weeks. My belief was that in my time of grief those 18 audiences were going to give me a great gift. In essence, I decided that if these beautiful people were going to give me the precious gift of their time, then the least I could do was to give them everything I had.

This has become my business philosophy. No matter whether I am speaking to a room of 30 people or to an audience of 3000 at the Convention Centre, if they give me their time, I owe it to them to give them everything I've got.

The same is true with individuals. When our child, partner, friend, colleague or customer gives us their time, it's our job to focus and give them our best attention and support.

Life is full of challenges

Gratitude leads to greater things

Let me ask you, do you spend most of your time thinking about all things that are wrong or all the things that you have going for you? Do you think about all the things you don't have or all the things you do?

Actually, forget about all the things you have. Some people may not have that much. That's actually not what is really important. Rather, do you think about all the things you don't have or do you think about all the *opportunities* you have? That's what really matters. It's about the opportunities that stretch out in front of you.

Sometimes there are people in the audience who have gone through tremendous loss financially that has affected how they see themselves. They may have lost everything and at 55 years old found themselves starting again. I say, 'Fantastic!' This is the best time in the history of the world to be 55 and broke! This is a useful belief about the reality, but it's also actually true. Imagine being 55 and broke in 1929. That would have been terrible! You might have ended up shovelling coal for a living. Today, there are opportunities everywhere.

I have had the privilege of meeting and talking with many successful people. I speak with a lot of people in their sixties and seventies who have climbed the mountain, sold their businesses and are sitting on their pot of gold. They have everything they thought they ever wanted. Yet, when they speak with me at the end of their career, more often than not they surprise me with their observations on the state of their lives. 'Chris,' they say, 'I thought it would feel different. I mean, it's nice to have all this. But actually, it's not as satisfying as I thought it would be.'

They discover that the joy is not in sitting on that pile of gold when they reach the top, but in *hunting* for the gold throughout their career. We are most alive when we are struggling, when we are in the middle of the battle of life. We are most alive when we are in the game. Many of these successful people just want to create a new challenge so they can get moving again.

Talk to most ex-professional athletes and get their perspective, even the ones who go on to have successful media careers. For them, they enjoy talking about the game, but nothing compares to being *in* the game. That's the joy. They spend the rest of their lives reminiscing about the big games, the big moments and shared experiences with teammates.

If I am speaking to an audience of 500 people, I might ask them all to name and think about the five things they are most proud of in their lives. Together we would compile a list of 2500 amazing accomplishments. Do you know what is really amazing about that list? Not one of those things we are really proud of came easily. Every single thing on that list was *hard*, challenging. Those are the things we are proud of. No one is proud of the things they've done that fell well inside their comfort zone.

If you talk to a 70-year-old person who is fully engaged in their life, you will find they are happy. If you talk to a 70-year-old who is sitting on their rocking chair on the veranda reminiscing about their lives, most of them are missing the action. They miss what drove them to success. We are happiest when we are in the midst of struggle, goal setting and accomplishment.

It's a given in our society that achieving a level of comfort in our lives will necessarily bring us joy. In reality, there is very little joy to be found in the comfort zone. People are most alive when they are dreaming and pushing themselves to achieve things beyond what they thought they were capable of. This is the best time in history to be alive, the best time in history to be you. Life begins at (insert your age). Now is the time to set new challenges in your life and be grateful for the opportunities ahead of you.

Think about the words we say to ourselves first thing in the morning to start our day. Do we use words that get us excited for the gift of a new day, or do we dwell on what a grind today is going to be? When you wake up tomorrow morning, note the first five, six, seven things you think about.

For most people this monologue will be along the lines of, *Damned alarm clock. Only Thursday! Ahhh, my head hurts. Why did I drink like that last night?* They drag themselves out of bed and think, *Man, my back is killing me today.* After taking two steps they think, *Actually it's not my back ... it's my feet. Must have been those new shoes.* They slip past their partner, who is still blissfully asleep, and shake their head with a deep sigh. They stumble into the shower and think about all of the day's deadlines and meetings, including that one-on-one with their boss.

Gratitude leads to greater things

That prompts another sigh and the thought, *Whatever, boss. Looking forward to all the criticism, ferret face!* Then out of the shower they look in the mirror for the first time. Which is where the real expletives begin!

The most important words we say all day are the words we say to ourselves, about ourselves when we are alone with ourselves. Most people are cruel in those moments. We need to be kind to ourselves. This is the best time to be in your job, in your career, and you look good today. Remember, you can change your reality, but if you're not going to change it or can't change it, you may as well have a useful belief about it.

So many people go through the week forgetting to live their lives and just holding out for the weekend. Wednesday is 'hump day', halfway home to when they can be happy again. Be careful of ideas like that. They are not useful. I hear people say that they live from holiday to holiday. They finish their holiday and the first thing they think is, *Just three more months until I get back to Bali again*. This is not useful.

Today is your launch pad

Bad things do happen to all of us. The sad reality is that relationships do end, sometimes acrimoniously. Jobs disappear, businesses fail. People we love pass away. We will face all sorts of adversity in the course of our lifetime, and it is important to consider some useful beliefs about the bad stuff as well as the good stuff. Let's look at a couple of useful beliefs for the course of our lives.

Everything that has happened in your life happened for a reason. Every single event that took place led you to exactly here, reading this book, right now. Most importantly, this is exactly the place you need to be right now to launch the rest of your life.

Is this true?

I don't know. As I've said I don't really subscribe to absolute truths, but I know this: the *idea* is useful. It means that everything that has happened to you had purpose. Through all of the victories and all of the pain, you learned and you grew, so now you are in just the right spot to move forward.

'Sorry, Chris, but I just don't believe that things happen for a reason!'

Okay, well let's try this then. You finished school and you got a job, which led you to the next one... then you met that person... then you got that tattoo (that was a mistake), which led to this relationship... then you got that job, where someone gave you this book... and here you are. Once again, it would be useful to believe that everything that happened to you had meaning.

Today is the best day ever to launch the rest of your life.

Useful thinking about tough decisions

Sometimes there are tough family decisions to make. People may make the choice to stay in a troubled relationship for all sorts of reasons—the kids, money, companionship and so on. It's okay. Stay, commit and find a useful belief about the people you live with. You make those decisions for a reason. It's not always going to be perfect. It's so easy to think that the grass is greener on the other side of the fence. Decide which side of the fence you are going to play on. After you decide, create a useful belief to support it.

At some stage you may make the decision that your relationship has reached the end of the line. Once again, there will be all sorts of reasons for deciding to wind it up. Sometimes quitting something that is not working in your life is the right thing to do. Life decisions can be complicated. But if you are going to change it, make sure you have a useful belief that supports your decision. Not everything works out, and that's okay.

Bitterness can eat us up. Often we try to stifle the chatter of insecurity, regret, disappointment or anger towards someone who has hurt us. That bitterness can manifest itself in our identity and create a pattern of victim behaviour that is paralysing or destructive.

Bad things happen to everyone. We have all known pain and had experiences that left us feeling resentful towards someone. Those painful experiences will vary widely in intensity and in the damage they cause. I don't want to start a competition on degrees of suffering. Rather, I'll state simply that when we are able to forgive people, we feel better. And that is useful.

When we stop attributing blame, we are free to focus on becoming the best version of ourselves. It is very useful to recognise that other people can only do what they were capable of at that time. Managing your expectations of other people can help you manage your own ability to let things go. Give some thought to how you could do a better job maintaining your personal health using forgiveness, managing expectations and letting go.

Perfection gets in the way of an outstanding life

There are parts of our lives that are truly important to us as human beings. It is important to know where to focus your attention. It would be great to put some useful thinking and useful beliefs around important things, but be careful not to set yourself up with the idea that your life needs to be somehow perfect in all these areas.

We are all most likely feeling like we are failing in some of the important areas of life. The reality is, for the most part, we are doing the best we can. Some are trying to be the perfect parent, the perfect partner, the perfect employee, the perfect manager or the perfect friend. Some are struggling to be a good husband after many years of trying. Others are trying to be a good wife, which, let's face it, is probably even harder because it's not like old guys are getting *less* gross!

Many of us get too busy with work, home and friends and all the obligations that go with them, then we fail to get to the gym, gain two kilos and are cruel to ourselves.

We are trying to be perfect in every area. This is of course impossible. Aiming for perfection inevitably makes us feel bad about ourselves.

It is this constant hankering for perfection that makes us feel guilty. This is not useful.

The pursuit of perfection gets in the way of living an outstanding life.

There, I said it. No more need to be perfect. When we try to be perfect at everything, we set ourselves up to fail. The pursuit of perfection actually makes us *less* perfect. If you walk in the door at night and expect everything in your life to be perfect, the first thing you will see is everything that is *wrong*.

This is something we need to deal with, because there are societal expectations of everyone that are unfair. We feel guilty when we get so busy at work that we are not home on time. Sometimes we are home or need to pick up the kids from school, and we can't actually do what we feel we are supposed to be doing. So we feel guilty because we're not at work. Sometimes we are absolutely overwhelmed with work *and* home. While trying to juggle all that, we beat ourselves up about it.

Then there are those who feel guilty about actually taking the personal time to go to yoga class. Heaven forbid that you take a little me time.

Let's do something that will eliminate the guilt from your life forever. That would be good. Let me introduce you to the tool that will get rid of this bad thing forever...

Perfection gets in the way of an outstanding life

Guilt is not your friend

10 seconds of guilt ... move on.

That's right, I want you to feel really bad for 10 seconds. Then I want you to leave the feeling behind you.

There are two situations involving guilt in which this can be used. The first is when we feel guilty about something we can't control. If we can't control it or change it, then feeling guilty is not going to help us or anyone else. It is not useful. The second scenario is if we feel guilty about not being perfect. We are all human, and sometimes things don't work out the way we want them to. We say the wrong thing, do the wrong thing or make a mistake. Take your 10 seconds and then ask yourself, 'What did I learn?'

My mother taught me this at a young age. I would walk into the house after school, devastated that I had failed a Year 8 maths test, and I'd say, 'Mom, I screwed up so bad. I'm such an idiot. I can't believe I failed that test!'

She would sit me on the couch and calm me down and we would talk through everything that had happened—what went well, what didn't. The talking through bit is important, by the way. Then she'd say, 'Now there's nothing we can do to change it. This is the reality. I do want you to feel bad about this. So feel bad for 10 seconds, then exit the feeling and move on.'

The 10 seconds is important because you have to be conscious of what you are feeling and that there's nothing you can do to change it. It is not useful to hang on to it.

Much later, I'd come home from a party in Year 11 and I'd say something like, 'Mom, I can't believe it. I said the stupidest thing. I was trying to pick up this girl, and now she hates me and I'm such a fool!' And of course she'd sit me down, and we'd go through the old process: 10 seconds of guilt…move on.

One time when I was telling this story to a large audience a woman raised her hand and said, 'Chris, can I make a comment?'

'Sure,' I said, 'of course.'

'Well, I was raised Irish Catholic. I'm going to need a lot longer than 10 seconds.'

The audience laughed.

'How long do you think you're going to need?' I asked.

'Well,' she said, 'I'm going to need at least seven minutes.'

'Fine,' I declared. 'Seven minutes of guilt … move on!'

While we're on the subject of guilt, we may as well talk about family. Family can be a tough one to have a useful belief about. Many people have a lot of pain here. One of my favourite useful beliefs is that we are all given the parents we are *supposed* to have.

What? Are you kidding me? You obviously haven't met my parents, Chris!

I know. Your parents may be pretty difficult or they may be great, or anywhere in between. However it works out, they are *your* parents. This is your reality, and there is nothing you can do to change it. So like everything you can't change, you may as well have a useful belief about it. No matter how you learned to cope with challenging family members, these experiences made you stronger.

It isn't useful to blame your parents for the past, painful experiences, or bad choices you made. The lessons you learned made you *stronger!* Use them. Be grateful for the lessons that were wins and turn the losses into celebrations. Be grateful they were your parents. Good or bad, learn from the experiences. It is useful to believe you were lucky to have been exposed to that wisdom.

And you survived! Congratulations. Now it's time to use that experience to make you powerful. No bitterness, no chip on the shoulder. Release. Congratulations on your strength. Sometimes the useful belief might be no more than that they did the best they could with what they knew at the time. They did the best they could given the pain *they* were in.

Sometimes family members disappoint us. We expect more from them yet they continually let us down. They might show glimmers of potential to be the loving mother, father, brother, sister or in-law that you want them to be, yet they end up disappointing you again and again. Much of the sadness around this is based on your expectations of others. When you accept the limits of what they are capable of, your expectations of them change. Your relationship may not be all you had hoped it would be, and that can be hard, but this useful belief will bring more peace to your heart.

Everyone has such different experiences with family. Some of us have large families with strong parents, and the pressure to please them all can be overwhelming. It feels like every one of them has a critical opinion of your business. Others have small families that share intimate, always supportive relationships. Still others have very distant relationships with their family.

Guilt is not your friend

No matter what your situation, it is important to have useful beliefs about the reality.

If you love your partner, and they bring you only happiness, congratulations! This is the best time in history to be in such a relationship. This too is a useful belief.

Another is that this is the best time ever to be single. It really is, though! Where was Tinder when I was 22?

This is also the best time in history to be a single parent. Children are remarkably adaptive, and sometimes the best thing you can do for them as parents is make a decision to change the situation. I'm not saying this is easy. I'm just saying that sometimes it's the reality, in which case the entire family needs to come up with a useful belief about it. This situation is hardly new. I am a child of divorced parents, and I know that sometimes this is the best decision for everyone. Things will work out as they should. Time is our friend, and over time everyone will come to see that this was the decision that needed to be made.

Whatever the situation, this is *your* story. Let's create a useful belief about it.

Forget work–life balance — it's a swing

Something I find truly fascinating is the way we rationalise decisions about the balance between work, family and money. You already know I travel a lot. To maintain the lifestyle of a professional speaker there are sacrifices that have to made both by me and by my family. It is certainly not a balance. I find it useful to think of it more as a swing.

For the professional speaker, there are times of the year that are busy and other times that are not. No one in Australia holds conferences in December or January, so I usually get a chance to take seven or eight weeks off then. That's perfect for me because it also aligns with school holidays. However, there are other times that I am far away when I would prefer not to be. Sometimes the swing is strong towards work and sometimes it is strong towards family. I have a useful belief that this is okay. This is the practical, necessary decision I've made.

There are no definitive rights or wrongs to this. I have spoken to many people who have made exactly the opposite choice to the decision I made. They passed up business opportunities so as not to be away from their family. Sometimes the promotion is not meant to be, and that's okay. Other opportunities will arise. Go through the process of useful thinking to make the decision.

Remember, modelling success for your children is hugely important. Children are more adaptive than you think they are. We live in a society today that somehow expects us to live and pay bigger bills than ever before yet still be home to micromanage every aspect of raising our children. Make the decision. Useful belief. Congratulations on your personal success.

For those young twentysomethings who just read the last few paragraphs, if you are obligation free in your life right now, my advice is to make the most of your freedom. This is the best time in history to work long hours and work your way into a successful situation. This is the best time in the history of the world to take that job overseas and push yourself and broaden your experience.

Many people feel they are shackled by responsibilities that can seem overwhelming. My objective is to help them reframe their reality so that it better serves them. However, if you have no responsibilities, don't shackle yourself when you don't need to. Go for it.

Living with making a living

Work is important. It is how we spend over a third of our life and is a huge part of our self-esteem. So it is really important to have some useful beliefs about work. It doesn't matter what the job is; what is important is the pride we take in it.

Pay attention to the language you use when you talk to yourself about work.

If your job is to dig a hole, dig the best hole possible. Pride in our work plays a huge role in how we see ourselves and our contribution to the world.

It is amazing how many people have belief systems about work that are not useful. Let's create some useful beliefs about the jobs we do. This is the best time to be in your business, at your company and in your industry. There are opportunities everywhere. Is this true? Once again, truth doesn't matter as much as we think it does. This is useful, and the reticular activating system will help you find those opportunities.

We hear a lot of nostalgic talk about other times that were better than today. They say, 'Things were different here in 2015!' or 'Oh, 2007, before the global financial crisis, was a great time to work here.' Sometimes they'll say, 'The nineties…they were good times! I could smoke at my desk!'

None of it matters. Other than enjoying a few moments of reflective sentiment, here's a quick news flash. It's not 2015, 2007 or 1996. It is right now, the best time in history to be in your industry and, with opportunities everywhere, the best time ever to be in your job.

A quick note on business and sales. I have had the privilege of working with hundreds of thousands of salespeople over the years. There is really only one thing above all else that distinguishes the best salespeople in the world from the average salespeople. The best salespeople see opportunities the others just don't see. They make money in any market. When you believe there is opportunity out there, your reticular activating system goes out there and finds it. When you believe these are tough times, your brain simply goes and finds all the reasons to believe in tough times. You will find all sorts of excuses about why things are not working out for you!

There are always opportunities everywhere. This is most certainly a useful belief.

Choose people who give you power

Real friends are a huge part of our life. I say *real* friends, not just your social media friends. Friends you can touch. This is hugely important in creating a life for yourself, away from family members. It is important to establish social outlets away from the potential stresses of family and work. It is useful to invest in these people.

Typically, women have done better than men at creating real and vulnerable relationships. Women do a better job of sustaining female relationships that give them companionship and strength. Men need to work on this. Especially in challenging times, men need to continue to get better at expressing themselves to each other and sharing. For generations, men have been taught that vulnerability is a sign of weakness. The truth is the opposite, of course.

It is important to surround yourself with people who give you power. It is time to get rid of the toxic people in your life. This may be the toxic co-worker who constantly fills your head with doom and gloom about the job. Or it may be the toxic person in your friendship group who slowly chips away at your confidence with comments that are designed to bring you down. The definition of a toxic person is someone who, after you spend time with them, leaves you feeling worse about yourself than before. You know that person. Maybe this is the year to let them go.

I hope that did not affect your marriage.

Fear vs anxiety

We are living in a time of unprecedented noise. Everyone is telling us they have the answers to all life's challenges, from running a business to running a family. I doubt you could count how many books there are on raising children. So many people with passionate, often diametrically opposed opinions, as though the human race had never raised children before.

Recently I was speaking with a counsellor friend of mine who has been working in that capacity with people of all ages for over 40 years. He blew me away one day when he recounted how, throughout the first half of his career, the problem of anxiety played a smaller role than it does today. Of course it was spoken about, but it wasn't really the obsession it has become today. He said they talked less of anxiety than of the idea of fear. I was sort of shocked by his observation.

This is a huge difference. It is completely different to fear something external than to blame yourself for the anxiety. Some people feared failure or of not living up to others' expectations. They feared the dark. Think about the difference. One is something external that we can all work towards overcoming and conquering. The other is internal, about our identity and the very fabric of who we are as a person. Today we are not so much afraid of anything specific, as generally anxious. This language implies that it is our fault!

We are living in a society that pronounces every day that it knows how we should behave and think in every aspect of our lives. With all these so-called experts (basically, anyone with an opinion), you would think we might have found better answers. Instead, we have the highest anxiety rates ever recorded.

I suggest that what we really have to define is the useful things to believe about our world and the useful activities for us to participate in.

It is easy to blame social media for our anxiety, as we all do to a greater or lesser extent. Even now some readers are thinking, *I'm really enjoying reading this book, but that smashed avocado I had for breakfast this morning was so great that I just had to post it on Instagram. And while I'm reading, I also feel tempted to put the book down to check how many likes I have on my smashed avocado!*

We're all dealing with so much stuff that it is increasingly important to think about what is useful and what is not. Which activities in your life are useful and which might you be better off getting rid of? What needs to be done and what needs to be delegated? I'm sure plenty of readers think that if an activity is to be done well they just have to do it themselves.

Ask yourself, what business activities are income producing and what are not? What are the activities that get results? What are the activities that get in the way of success? What do you need to start doing, and what do you need to stop doing? Which do you need to do more of and which less of?

What are your useful beliefs in every sphere of your life?

Avoid outside broadcasts

Obviously there are a lot of toxic people stalking social media. That pool of judgement that we constantly jump into in the hope that we will be loved and accepted, that our latest post will be met with raving affirmation and praise. This sets us up to feel bad about ourselves.

Social media will never replace the bonds of real friendship. It cannot come close to the face-to-face experience of listening, responding and sharing with someone we love and care about. But it has become almost impossible to talk about friends in the modern world without addressing the power of this new-world communication and its effects on our psychology.

Social and other media bombard us with messages about the sort of body we should have, the products we should own and the experiences we should be brave enough to embrace. It would be easy to make the claim that it has always been so. Advertising has always exhorted us to envy and emulate the beautiful people, products and lifestyles, most of which are virtually unattainable for the majority.

Today, though, we have the opportunity to do our own advertising, to broadcast our life directly to the world. For many of us this is exciting, because we can share our greatest moments and get direct feedback on them. We also get to snap and upload holiday photos of our pool view, cocktail, beautiful meal and beach walk, as though we were celebrities.

I have to say I really enjoy most of this. It's fun to see what people I know around the world are doing at the moment, allowing for time differences of course. While I live in Australia, my mum can instantly see the pictures of our Thailand holiday from her home in Colorado. Also, it is an amazing boon for business to be able to communicate messages to thousands of people at a time.

There are two risks to be aware of, though:

1 Needing your life to be perfect creates a massive amount of anxiety.
2 Comparing yourself to others creates a massive amount of anxiety.

Double and triple check that your self-esteem is not tied too closely to the number of likes you receive on an average post. None of us are perfect, and perceived perfection is actually not an attractive quality. It is easy to resent people whose lives seem so perfect. We are much more attracted to a level of vulnerability in people that makes them authentic.

Be real. You do not have to look like Ryan Gosling or Blake Lively. Simply be the best version of yourself. The more your social media reflects your true self, the less stressed you will be. The further it moves away from the real you, the more attached you will be to the feedback you get.

A few years ago I made up a word and for fun posted it. The word was 'wankxious'. The definition was 'when I'm considering posting something then stop and think to myself, "If I post this will I be thought a wanker?"'. This makes me wankxious!

Your body reflects your mind

When I am talking on stage about useful beliefs and the useful actions that follow, it is important to convey how this all manifests itself in the body. There is something called the Mind-Body Loop. Useful beliefs affect your thoughts and change your perception of how you view the world. Those thought patterns and beliefs, in turn, influence your body. By the same token, how you move your body affects what you think about. What the mind harbours, the body will manifest.

Healthy people have better posture than sick people, but also sad people. Successful people stand taller and move more confidently than people who feel they are failing. If you watch someone with excellent posture, you'll notice that their body language conveys they are alert and awake. Make no mistake, the mind follows suit. When the body is alert and awake, the mind too is alert and awake.

Successful people hold themselves in a certain way. In meetings and at conferences you can identify powerful leaders by their distinctive posture. Carry yourself in a way that demonstrates that you intend to be successful! I see so many people sitting at the weekly meeting so slumped over they can barely hold themselves up.

How do you present yourself in company and sales meetings? How do you sit at training sessions? How do you walk into the office first thing each morning? How do you carry yourself when you walk through the front door at home at the end of a hard day? What about when you go to the gym for a workout? What posture do you assume when your children want your attention?

Other people in your life will respond to the physical posture you adopt when you approach them. Therefore, consider whether the body language you're exhibiting is useful. Not only can this improve your interactions with other people, but it will change your personal mindset through the Mind-Body Loop. What the mind harbours, the body manifests. Be sure you adopt useful body language.

Keep your eyes open

Do you believe that the eyes are the window to the soul?

Eyes can be pretty amazing. I can be standing on stage and catch the eye of someone in the audience and immediately feel the intensity with which they are listening. I can feel how fully they are engaged in what I'm saying. Their eyes create an instant connection.

When you have a useful belief, you are able to be more present and enjoy the moment. Being present is one of the key benefits of useful belief.

So often people have their thoughts focused on a different time frame. Sometimes that means being so focused on the completion of a goal that they fail to be present in the now and enjoy the task at hand. Other times it can mean being so focused on the way things used to be done around here that they are unable to deliver or even understand how things need to be done today.

It is amazing how many parents are not present for their children. The child walks into the room and says, 'Dad, look at the picture I drew.' Her father, who is busy in the kitchen, never really makes eye contact with her. Instead, he glances fleetingly over his shoulder and responds with a distracted 'That's great, sweetie, but right now I've got to get dinner ready.' He didn't really look at the picture, or his daughter, which means he missed an opportunity to connect. He might have squatted down beside her, looked her in the eyes and said, 'That's beautiful, that's fantastic,' but he missed the moment.

It's the same in almost any relationship. People get busy, they forget to focus on and make eye contact with the people they love. Your partner walks in and says, 'Hey, honey! How was your day?' You smile while checking your email on your phone and reply, 'Good … good. Let me just quickly finish this and I'll be with you.'

It happens all the time. When you fail even to make eye contact, you are not really present. Making eye contact and being present are useful actions, a product of having a useful belief about whatever activity you are doing.

How present are you? How good are you at looking at people directly and making the kind of eye contact that lets them know you are really listening to them and not distracted by other thoughts or activities? Being present is very useful in the art of influencing others.

It's okay to smile

Sometimes people see the word smile come up on the screen at my keynote presentations and I know they think to themselves, *What? Smile? How simplistic is that? This is like some 1980s motivational seminar.*

Well, no, it's not. I do a great impression of a 1980s motivational speaker, though. Imagine that American accent ringing out, saying, 'When you smile at the customer, the customer feels real goooood. In fact, it's not just when you are face to face. Put a smile on that dial and you can send that smile straight down the phone line and the customer will feel that smile at the other end. Remember, customers want to deal with people they like.'

It's a pretty good impression when I do it on stage. But even though it sounds facile to talk about the power of smiling, I still have to bring it up—for one huge reason. When you smile at another person, it makes them feel good about…who? *Themselves.*

Think about that for a second. Smiling at another person makes them feel good about themselves. Imagine if someone came up to me and said, 'Chris, I have a new product that will instantaneously make other people—customers, colleagues and family members—feel good about themselves.'

I would personally pay millions of dollars for the product, sell it around the world and make a fortune. The thing is, of course, we already have it. If smiling at others makes them feel good about themselves, it stands to reason that *not* smiling at another person is a selfish act!

Living in Melbourne I have noticed a really sad trend that seems to me continues to worsen. People are forgetting to smile at each other as their paths cross. I'll be walking my dog and passing people on the footpath and they look down. We're not greeting and smiling at each other. What's happening? How hard is it to smile and say hello?

It's no different with customers. People want to deal with people that they like. We have the ability to instantaneously make people feel good about themselves, yet we are always so busy. People are so consumed with the stress and anxieties of the modern world that we are forgetting to exercise basic human courtesy. It is symptomatic of the self-focused world we live in. If you want to increase your likeability, it's a short trip. Start smiling and notice how people treat you differently. That is most useful.

It's okay to smile

Some conclusions

He or she who shoots at nothing generally hits it.

Let me ask you a question. Have you ever felt like a day, a week or a month goes by, and next thing you know six months have passed, and you're not actually sure if you are moving in the right direction? Are you getting closer or further away from what you want to achieve in your life? Are you getting closer to your *sunset*?

What sunset, you ask? Great question. The sunset here is a metaphor for a clear future. It is a metaphor that will drive your useful beliefs, and that will guide the development of your identity, behaviours and results in life. How does this work?

Before I go into it, I want you to know that I just love a sunset. West coast sunsets are the best. California, Bali and Perth are among my favourites. I love that moment when the sun touches the horizon. I imagine it will take a while before it submerges into the water, but it doesn't. It seems like a few seconds and it's gone. I love that moment.

It is a moment when I have clarity about the day that has just slipped into the ocean. A time to reflect on the day. What went well, what didn't? What did we learn? What will we do again? What will we try to avoid tomorrow?

The good news is we can also go time travelling with this idea of the sunset to gain clarity about our lives. This is useful. We can even visit the future and gain clarity about what we really want to achieve. Imagine, for example, travelling one year into the future and walking up to me and saying, 'Chris, I have had the best year of my life. Personally, professionally, physically, my relationships. This has been the best 12 months ever!'

I ask you, how did that come about? What did you start doing, stop doing and keep doing? This will give you clarity about exactly what you need to do.

A lot of people try to set goals by living in the moment, and that's a problem. Many people live and work on what I call the hamster wheel of life. That hamster is going round and round, working really hard, but really making no progress in any specific direction? These people are the same.

They get up every day, work hard, running on and on inside that hamster wheel. At the end of the day they are tired, but they have actually made little or no progress towards where they want to go in their life. They aren't reaching the level of accomplishment they had hoped for. Often they aren't even sure they're running on the right hamster wheel.

The problem is they are just *reacting* to what's happening in the present.

Instead, let's create your sunset. You want to go time travelling into the future. Imagine it's three months from now and you are calling your best friend to say, 'I've never been happier in my job than I am right now. I've never been more connected to my business than I am right now.' What would it take to get you to the place where you could say those words? What could have happened between now and then? What did you do? What did you put in place? The answers to these questions indicate the actions you need to take.

Let's look at health and the changes you could make there in the next six months. To walk into a room six months from now and be proud of how you look, how you feel, how you are connected to yourself, what did you change? The answer points to the action you need to take.

It's no different over a longer time span. I am always fascinated to talk with older people in their eighties and nineties. I love asking them about their lives. The decisions they made. I find that people in the sunset of their lives describe them in one of two ways. Some have a sense of fulfilment. They tell you about their kids and grandkids. If they never had kids, they tell you about the work and the travel and the relationships they have experienced. They describe their life with a sense of contentment.

Sadly, though, most people look back on their lives with regret. It's interesting, though. It's not the mistakes they made that they regret. It's not the things they did. It's the things they *didn't* do.

Imagine sitting in your favourite chair, glass of wine in hand, in front of an open fire, looking back over the events of your life and reflecting on everything that happened. You'll want to look back and say to yourself, *I have loved my life. I've lived my life the way I wanted to live it. I feel fulfilled.* To reach the point where you feel that way about your life, what did you do? What risks did you take? No regrets. These are the kinds of actions you need to take.

I've always been fascinated by the idea of sliding door moments, and how the direction of our life can change radically in one moment as a result of one seemingly unimportant decision or circumstance. Make a different choice then and life might be altered forever.

Many people out there have made choices in their lives that they regret. These regrets often cause them to develop a chip on their shoulder. Everyone goes through this to some degree, but some people experience it much more acutely than others. It suffocates them, frustrating opportunities for future success and possibility. Other people have fewer regrets and don't hold on to feelings of guilt or insecurity as tightly as others.

These regrets may have been around decisions about what to study, whom to marry, whether or not to have children, choice of profession, moving away from family and friends — the list goes on and on. Some will tell me those decisions were the best things they ever did. Others will describe these moments, the decisions and the circumstances in which they were made, with tremendous regret.

Often those sliding door moments and the corresponding choices are not even ours to make. Everyone can tell you of situations in which they had no control or power. Things people said to you or did to you, the people who decided not to love you or who left you by passing away.

All of these moments, decisions and circumstances are critical in defining the emotional baggage each person carries around with them. The more time people play in the arena of past regrets, the harder it is for them to live in the now or gain clarity about the future. Instead, they live their lives focused on the past and events they cannot change. This is not useful. It is virtually impossible to influence others until you are able to master your own timeline. To do that, these regrets need to be transformed into opportunities for *learning*.

Whenever something significant happens in your life, ask yourself two simple questions: Why did this happen? What have I learned from it?

It is amazing how answering these two questions can take any significant negative event in your life and turn it into a useful lesson. When asked these questions, your brain can't help but search for a useful response for why a certain event happened and what you learned from it. This useful thinking leads to an acceptance of your life and your reality.

I challenge you to do this with each of the regrets you have over moments, decisions and circumstances in your past. Ask yourself those two questions. Because it is an incredible thing when you feel the weight of past regrets lift off your shoulders, so instead of oppressing you they now make you stronger. That belief is incredibly useful.

Too many people live much of their lives focused on the negative past. Be very careful to use the past as a source of learning rather than getting sucked into the 'woulda, coulda, shoulda'. When you turn the negative past into learning, it will no longer hold you back. Instead, it will serve as a guide to making better decisions, living in the now and moving confidently towards the future.

I have had the opportunity to meet so many amazing people. Sometimes I meet someone who possesses a quality I like to think of as a calm presence. It just feels like they are so in control of being and acting in a way that is congruent with who they are as a person. They are truly present and comfortable in their own skin. They are really good at just being themselves.

The truth is our lives change. Healing comes when we move forward. It is about using the lessons from the past to create a better future. It is also about our determination to be a better person ten years from now than we are today.

Business is no different. The reality is, here too the past is gone. That chapter is closed. For many people, the way they did business in years gone by may not work today. The approaches they used in the past may not generate business and customer loyalty the way they once did. But they have some options. They can look at their current situation and ask themselves what they want to do about it.

I challenge you to spend some time on this. Discover what your future is really all about. For you to be the person you really want to be, what new behaviours do you need to put in place? What new habits do you need to adopt? Pay attention to the patterns of language you use when speaking about the past. There is nothing wrong with remembering the good times, but it is more important that you jump with both feet into a new, useful reality.

What is going to work today? What do you need to get rid of from your past? Tell your story in a way that gives you power.

Make yourself the hero of your own story.

A summary of useful ideas

We are all overwhelmed by a constant avalanche of information about just about everything. A lot of it is not useful and is simply noise. With useful belief thinking, we identify the things we should pay attention to and those we should not.

Most people don't need transformation but, rather, a simple shift that opens the door to how they view their reality.

Positive thinking doesn't really work by itself. Useful belief thinking does. Positive is emotional, while useful is practical.

Truth doesn't always matter as much as we think it does. As children we were taught a lot of things that were supposedly true. As adults, we discover that they often turned out not to be true at all. We can control our perceptions and decide what is a useful belief to have.

Our brain uses a filter, called the reticular activating system, that plays a part in deciding on the important information that should reach our consciousness. You can control whether your filter is helping you seek opportunities or relegating your thinking to seeking out tough times.

We all have a reality. We can change it. However, if there are things about our reality that we either can't or won't change, it is important to come up with useful beliefs about them.

Asking the question, 'What is the most useful thing for me to do today?' will make you more productive and help you achieve greater connection in your life. What is useful? What is not? What gets you results and what doesn't?

When other people give us their time, it is useful to believe that this is the greatest gift they could possibly give us. It is therefore our job to be present and to control our output. It is important that we give it everything we can in these moments.

Useful belief works best when you drive from the heart, not the ego. The heart doesn't judge.

Bad things happen to good people. And while grief is part of the healing process, at what point is it no longer useful? You can create a useful belief about past events in your life to better serve you. What did you learn? How did this make you more resilient and stronger?

Every single thing that happened in your life led to your reading this book, which is exactly the book you are supposed to read to launch the rest of your life. This is your story.

There is a three-part method to creating a useful belief. First, consider your situation. Give some thought to what it is that you want. Second, do some useful thinking. Consider all the useful beliefs to determine what sits best with you. Finally, create a useful belief you can believe in. Then be okay with that decision.

Gratitude is the cornerstone of useful belief. Watch how life changes for you when you focus on all the opportunities and adventures that lie ahead of you.

Energy is a decision. Most people are tired. You have energy when you are connected with your life. You are tired when you are disconnected from your life. How do you get connected? Simple. Have a useful belief about the things that you can't or won't change. Or change them! But if you're not going to change them, you may as well have a useful belief about them.

A summary of useful ideas

Don't try to be perfect. None of us are perfect. The pursuit of perfection gets in the way of living an outstanding life.

Guilt is not useful, so adopt the principle of '10 seconds of guilt ... move on!' Bring the feeling of guilt into your conscious awareness, then release it.

You had the parents you were supposed to have. Create a useful belief about your story.

We feel better when we are able to forgive others. It is useful to believe that people can only do what they are capable of. This helps us empathise with others and understand their failings.

The Mind-Body Loop plays an important role in our lives. What the mind harbours, the body will manifest. How you think affects how you move. How you move affects how you think.

Gain clarity about your sunset. This is your life. Tell your story in a way that gives you power. You are the hero of your story.

A list of useful beliefs referenced in this book

1   This is the best time in the history of the world to be alive!

2   This is the best time in the history of the world to be a kid.

3   This is the best time in the history of the world to be a parent.

4   There are always opportunities everywhere.

5   This is the best time in the history of the world to be at my company and in my industry.

6   Life begins at [insert your age].

7   I look good today.

8   I love challenging people and situations.

9   I love airplanes! I love airports! I love hotels and hotel sheets!

10   This is the best time in the history of the world to be alone.

11   The greatest gift people can give me is their time. When people give me their time, the least I can do is to give them everything I can.

A list of useful beliefs referenced in this book

12   Every single thing in your life happened for a reason and led to your reading this book. And this is exactly the moment for you to launch the rest of your life.

13   Bad things happen to good people. Grief is useful.

14   After enough time has passed, there is a point at which grief ceases to be useful. What did you learn? How can we turn this event into a celebration of life and learning?

15   The joy of life is not sitting on that pile of gold; it is hunting for the gold that makes us feel alive.

16 Struggle is good. The accomplishments we are most proud of in our life were hard won.

17 Life is a gift.

18 Today is a gift.

19 Energy is a decision. I can draw on as much energy as I want.

20 Pursuit of perfection gets in the way of living an outstanding life.

21 Guilt is not useful. Allow yourself 10 seconds of guilt ... move on.

22 I had the parents I was supposed to have.

23 It is important to make sacrifices for my family. [if applicable]

A list of useful beliefs referenced in this book

24   This is the best time in the history of the world to be a single parent. [if applicable]

25   This is the best time in the history of the world be single. [if applicable]

26   This is the best time in the history of the world to be in a relationship. [if applicable]

27   I can't change other people if they don't want to change.

28   There are other soul mates out there for you.

29   It is good to forgive others, even if they don't appreciate it.

30   People can only do what they are capable of. Manage your expectations of what others are actually capable of.

31   Social media is fun, but be sure to be real, to be authentic.

32   Work is important, and taking pride in my accomplishments is important.

33   Modelling success for my children is important.

34   There are business opportunities everywhere out there.

35   This is the best time in history to go out and make money.

A list of useful beliefs referenced in this book

36   This is the best time in history
      to be 55 and broke. There are
      opportunities everywhere to
      start again!

37   Being vulnerable is good and
      healthy. I drive from the heart.

38   If I can't change it or won't
      change it, I may as well have a
      useful belief about it.